What Birds Do and Say
An Ornithological Primer for the
Young and Young at Heart

Rohan — Happy Birding!
— Anne McCallum

Anne Kapler McCallum

LANIER
PRESS

LANIER PRESS *an Imprint of BookLogix*

Alpharetta, GA

ISBN: 978-1-61005-856-8

Library of Congress Control Number: 2017935915

10 9 8 7 6 5 4 3 2   0 3 2 8 1 7

Printed in the United States of America

♾This paper meets the requirements of ANSI/NISO Z39.48-1992 (Permanence of Paper)

Text and illustrations by Anne McCallum

Preface

Baby birds hatch from eggs, grow feathers, and learn to fly. How different they are from us people! But wait—birds also need to find food, water, shelter, and raise a family. That's not so different from us. In fact, birds do many of the same things we do, and some of them may surprise you!

Baby birds all seem to say, "Cheep cheep cheep," but each kind of grown-up bird has its own special sound. These sounds help people tell one kind of bird from another. Some sounds are beautiful, some are funny, and some are gross—just like people sounds.

What birds do and say is pretty amazing!

Her: Oo-eek! Oo-eek! Oo-eek!

Him: Seeeee–seeee–seeee!

All birds have feathers, and only birds have feathers. Feathers are great for warmth, protection, and flying, but they need constant care. When birds are not flying, eating, or sleeping, they are often **preening**—cleaning and combing their feathers. (They use their bills, not a comb!) Ducks also oil their feathers to make them waterproof. Neat, healthy, colorful feathers help birds, like this male Wood Duck, attract mates.

Wood Duck

Bob white! Bob white!

The Northern Bobwhite's spotty, brown feathers help it hide in its favorite **habitat**, brushy grasslands. Sometimes, hiding doesn't work and an enemy gets too close. Then the bobwhite usually runs away on its quick, little legs. But brown feathers and quick legs can't help when its habitat is destroyed. The bobwhite was once common in the eastern United States. Now, sadly, it is disappearing as small farms with pastures and woodlots are replaced by big farms and thick forests.

Northern Bobwhite

Ah-ooo-ooo-ooo-eeeee!

ah-ooo-ooo-ooo-eeeee!

hahahahaha!

In summer, the Common Loon's mysterious, laughing song echoes far across northern lakes. As the days grow shorter and cooler, it **molts**, replacing its striking black-and-white feathers with dull, gray ones. Then it **migrates** to spend the winter along the Atlantic or Pacific coast or on a large, ice-free lake. It rarely sings until it gets back to its northern nesting area in the spring. There, once again, it sings and looks sharp in its black-and-white feathers.

Common Loon

Grr . . . grngh . . . groink . . .

Grngh . . . grrrngh.

The Double-crested Cormorant has dark, glossy feathers. Unlike a duck, it has very little oil on its feathers. This makes it easier to dive deep in the water to catch fish, but its feathers get all wet when it dives. To dry off, the cormorant stands around on rocks and tree branches with its wings spread wide.

Double-crested Cormorant

Keow! Keow!

Skeow skeow skeow!

Kuckkuckkuckkuckkuck.

Birds find and eat many kinds of food. Herons and egrets are great at fishing. They wait patiently, then grab or stab a fish with their long, sharp bills and swallow it headfirst and whole. The Green Heron sometimes takes this a step further. It actually tosses out bait, such as insects, worms, or even small pieces of bread, to lure fish in close.

Green Heron

Hssgh! Hsssgh . . . grssh! Gruunghsssh!

Birds in the vulture family eat **carrion**—the rotting meat from dead animals. One vulture, the California Condor, is among the largest and rarest birds in North America. Up close, its bald head may look ugly to us, but there is a reason for it. While the condor is poking around inside a dead animal, its bald head stays neat and clean. Head feathers would get messy with bits of rotten meat and blood. From a distance, the condor looks elegant and majestic as it soars effortlessly on wings that measure nine feet from tip to tip!

California Condor

Keek-eek-eek-eek!

The super eyesight of eagles and hawks makes them very good **predators**. They may have the sharpest eyes of any animal—far better than human eyes. They are especially good at identifying moving objects that are very small or far away. They can spot a rabbit in a field half a mile away. They can see a fish under the surface of water. In fact, this is the Bald Eagle's favorite food.

Bald Eagle

Killdeer!

Killdeer!

Killdeer!

Birds have to find lots and lots of food when they have hungry babies to feed. They also need to keep their babies from becoming food for other animals! The Killdeer often uses the **broken-wing trick** to distract predators. It thrashes around on the ground pretending to be injured, all the while leading the predator farther and farther away from its nest or chicks. The predator may think it has a sure meal, but then the parent bird flies up and away. Pretty soon, it is back to the job of feeding its young.

Killdeer

Caw! Caw! Caw!

Ha-ha-ha-ha-ha-ha-ha!

A Herring Gull will eat just about anything: fresh fish, rotten fish, fresh clams, rotten clams, fried clams, eggs, baby birds, your lunch, my lunch, our garbage, worms, mice from plowed fields, and even sewage! Herring Gulls are almost as common around landfills as around lakes and oceans. Birds like this are called **scavengers**. Even though this gull can be annoying at a beach picnic, its eating habits help to keep our environment tidy and healthy.

Herring Gull

Who cooks for you?

Who cooks for you all?

Some birds do interesting things after they eat. A Barred Owl eats mice and other little animals whole, but it can't digest the fur and bones. This would be a problem for us, but the owl has a way to solve it. It coughs up the "leftovers" as **pellets**. We can take these pellets apart to find out what the owl had for lunch!

Barred Owl

Hmmmmmmmmmmmm.
Squeak squeak!

Hmmmmmmmmmmmm.
Squeak squeak squeak!

Hmmmmmmm . . .
SQUEAK SQUEAK SQUEAK!
@^#$%&!!*

Tiny Ruby-throated Hummingbirds live on flower **nectar** and small insects. Like many birds, they migrate south in the fall before their food supply disappears for the winter. They eat so much before their journey that they get fat. They almost double their weight! Then they have enough energy to fly nonstop across the Gulf of Mexico to tropical lands where they can sip nectar all winter.

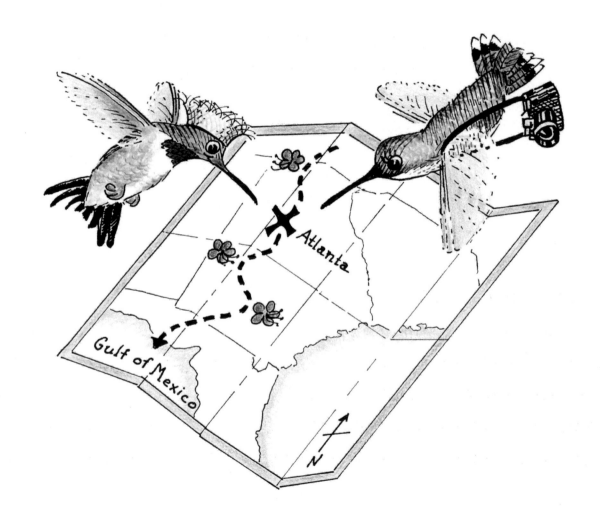

Ruby-throated Hummingbird

Kek! Kek!

Kekekekekekekekekekekekek!

Carpintero is the Spanish name for both "carpenter" and "woodpecker." The name fits this bird well, because it is constantly working with wood. It chisels out insects to eat. It carves holes in which to nest, or **roost**. It even drums on hollow trees to send messages! The big Pileated Woodpecker leaves large, deep nest holes that other animals may later use as their own homes.

Pileated Woodpecker

Tcher! Tcher!

Bubbleubbleubbleubble twittwit bubbleubbleubble tchertcher!

Cavity nesters are birds that build their nests in holes. The holes can be cavities made by woodpeckers, hollows formed by decay in trees, or birdhouses made by people. **Colony** nesters build their nests in a group close to each other. Purple Martins are both cavity nesters and colony nesters, so they love the apartment-like birdhouses that people provide. Birdhouse living isn't a new habit for them. Hundreds of years ago, they learned to nest in hollow gourds provided by Native Americans. Now they are so used to birdhouses that they seldom nest in natural cavities anymore.

Purple Martin

Chickadeedeedee.

Chickadeedeedee.

Upside down. Right side up. It doesn't matter to the acrobatic chickadees. These noisy little balls of energy will make a home wherever they can find seeds or small insects to eat. They are nonmigratory birds. They often roam the winter woods in mixed flocks with titmice, nuthatches, kinglets, and other small birds. To keep warm on cold winter nights, a small group of them huddles together in a hollow tree or even a birdhouse!

Carolina Chickadee

Teakettle, teakettle, teakettle-tea!
or
Teakettle, teakettle, teakettle, teakettle!
or twenty other loud songs.

Just building a nest is not enough to make a home for most birds. They also have to defend a **territory** that contains enough food to raise a family. The beautiful bird **songs** we enjoy are one way for a male bird to claim his territory. Even though the Carolina Wren is a very small bird, its song is very big. Its loud, ringing "teakettle, teakettle, teakettle!" fills the woods and swamps where it lives. It is telling other males to stay away. It is telling females that it has found a great place to live. Both male and female birds also make shorter **calls** and **chip notes** to scare off attackers, to warn of danger, and just to stay in touch.

Carolina Wren

Cheerily, cheer-up, cheerily.

Cheerily, cheer-up, cheerily.

People love birds for their songs, their colorful feathers, and their amazing ability to fly. People also love birds as signs of the changing seasons. All across the northern states, people watch for their first American Robin to tell them that spring is coming. The robin uses mostly grass and mud to build its nest, but it also reuses many materials that people have left outdoors. It might even build its nest on part of a building instead of in a tree.

REDUCE!
REUSE!
RECYCLE!

American Robin

Drop it. Drop it. Cover it up. Cover it up. Pull it up. Pull it up. Pull it up.

—Henry David Thoreau

In 1928, the schoolchildren of Georgia selected the Brown Thrasher as their **state bird**. More than forty years later, in 1970, the grown-ups in the state legislature finally made it official. All of the states and the District of Columbia have an official bird. The most popular ones are the Northern Cardinal (seven states), the Western Meadowlark (six states), and the Northern Mockingbird (five states).

Brown Thrasher

Chipchipchipchipchipchipchip chipchipchipchipchipchip.

Chipchipchipchipchipchipchip chipchipchipchipchipchip.

People have destroyed the habitats of many birds by building more and more houses and roads and shopping centers. But Chipping Sparrows seem to like our yards and parks, where they hunt for seeds and insects in the very short grass. Chippies are very little, brown birds, so it is easy to overlook them. But if you do see one, look around for more. They usually travel and feed in small **flocks**.

Chipping Sparrow

What! What! What cheer, cheer, cheer, cheer.
or
Purty, purty, purty, purty!

Another bird that likes places where people live is the Northern Cardinal. The male's bright-red feathers and pointed crest make it a favorite at bird feeders. The cardinal is not afraid of the winter cold. It will stay in the same area year-round as long as it can find food. Scientists believe that bird feeders have helped the cardinal expand its **range** several hundred miles north over the years.

Backyard Bistro
• black oil sunflower seed
• millet
• cracked corn
• peanuts
safflower seed
suet

Northern Cardinal

Spring of the year!
Spring of the year!

Both the Eastern and Western Meadowlark have a black "bib" of feathers, but they can't take it off after they eat! **Birders**, or **birdwatchers**, call patterns of colored feathers like this **field marks**. **Field guides** are books that use field marks to help birders tell one kind of bird from another. Birders also use **checklists** to keep track of all the birds they see. The birds in field guides and checklists are arranged in a special order—the same order you have been following in reading this book!

Eastern Meadowlark

Glossary

Birder or birdwatcher: A person who watches birds for fun rather than as part of a job.

Broken-wing trick: The way a bird leads a predator away from its nest or young by faking an injury.

Call and chip note: The sounds (usually less musical than the songs) made by both male and female birds to scare off attackers, to warn of danger, to show they are scared, or to stay in touch.

Carrion: The rotting meat of a dead animal.

Cavity: A hole or hollow place. Some birds nest in a cavity, usually one in a hollow tree.

Checklist: A list of the birds, other animals, or plants in a specific area.

Colony: A group of birds nesting together.

Field guide: A book used to identify birds, insects, animals, plants, trees, etc.

Field mark: An area of color or other visible feature that helps us tell one bird species from another.

Flock: A group of birds that travels and feeds together.

Habitat: A place that provides everything that a plant or animal needs. A bird's habitat has its food, water, hiding places, and nest sites.

Migrate: To move from one place to another with the change in seasons.

Molt: To shed old feathers and grow new ones.

Nectar: The sweet juice inside a flower that attracts butterflies, bees, and hummingbirds.

Pellet: A small ball of fur, bones, and other parts of a bird's food that it cannot digest. The bird coughs up pellets after eating.

Predator: A bird or other animal that hunts and eats other animals.

Preen: To clean, straighten, and oil feathers.

Range: The large general area a certain kind of bird lives in. Migratory birds have a summer range and a winter range.

Roost: To settle down for a bird nap or night's sleep.

Scavenger: A bird who helps clean up the environment by eating carrion.

Song: The musical sounds made most often by a male bird to announce its territory and to attract a mate. (See **call and chip note**.)

State bird: An official bird chosen to represent a state. The District of Columbia also has an official bird.

Territory: The small area within its range and habitat that an individual pair of birds occupies.

Acknowledgments

Thank you, thank you, thank you! So many people helped me get this book together. Atlanta Audubon (especially Catharine Kuchar and Nikki Belmonte) started it all in 2010 with a request—and suggestions—for bird cartoons. Those six original drawings became the core of a gift for my wonderful, nature-loving dad. That was "Clem Kapler's Bird Book." His enthusiasm prompted additions. I have had four super "critics" all along the way—little sister (and, conveniently, an editor in real life) Jane Smith, astute and ever-honest sons, Chuck and Eddie McCallum, and birder-buddy John E. Duke. I'm also grateful to the many innocent bystanders who (if they expressed any interest at all) found themselves reading the book, often more than once, and made many useful suggestions—especially Charlie Muise and my fellow "Band Aides" at the Panola Mountain Bird Banding Station. Georgann Schmalz graciously agreed to look it over for ornithological correctness. Linda Bernard kindly did the final prep work to send it off to publishers. My very professional, talented, and thorough team at Lanier Press polished it off and saw it through the publishing process.

And, of course, super hubby and encourager Jim did everything from posing with needed objects in his primaries—oops, I mean hands—to photographing backgrounds to photoshopping away my blunders.

I appreciate all of you! And above all, thanks to God for the birds of the air that He has given us to enjoy and to protect!

About the Author

As a girl, Anne Kapler McCallum started watching birds with her family from the kitchen window of their home in Cresco, Iowa. She studied art and English in college and graduate school and spent summers watching birds while working at national parks in the West. After she retired from thirty-five years of teaching English, Anne is now able to spend more time with the birds: watching them, helping with bird banding, and drawing them—especially for the Atlanta Audubon Society. She and her husband, Jim, have two grown sons and live in Clayton County, Georgia, where they enjoy watching birds from the kitchen window.